The Commandments of Lacrosse

50 Rules to follow to make yourself a better teammate and player of the game!

David Gardner

The Commandments of Lacrosse

All Commandments were first given to me somehow, by someone I do not remember. I have researched for an original author, but without luck. You can find these on multiple Lacrosse related websites throughout the internet and I do not claim to have originally come up with them. I have always provided this to my players at the end of the season as a means to help them develop their skills as a better teammate and lacrosse player, but felt they were lacking in direction and suggestions. Around 2010, I turned these rules into an audio series that you can grab at the website BasicLacrosse.com and find out about other cool lacrosse things, as well as be the first to know when updates or new editions of this book come out.

I have added on to each commandment with extra tips, strategies and suggestions in various cases to help understand the concepts better.

Published 2012: Independently through CreateSpace.com in association with BasicLacrosse.com and LacrosseCommandments.com

Republished and updated 2022

Have questions or comments, send them to me here:

Dave Gardner
110 Gulino Ave
Camillus, NY 13031

DaveGardner@BasicLacrosse.com

Written and Video Reviews or testimonials are greatly appreciated!
LacrosseCommandments.com/Blog/bookreview

The Commandments of Lacrosse

Basic Lacrosse Disclaimer

Lacrosse can be a brutal sport and it is crucial that the necessary precautions are set in place to provide a safe environment to play in, including being properly equipped.

Your stick should be checked before practice for stringing issues and cracks...not during line drills.

Your equipment should also be checked for loose straps and buckles, especially on the helmet or goggles. If you have a crack or tear in something, chances are it is time for a new one and you should show your coach or an official to get their advice.

Remember, safety comes first and we do not want an injury to plague the rest of the season or even your life.

The Commandments of Lacrosse

Introduction

The Creator's game has continued to evolve since first being introduced by the Native American Indian tribes hundreds of years ago. There have been numerous names for the game such as Stick Ball, Baggataway, or Tewaaraton, which means "Little Brother of War" and is also the name of the award given to the modern player of the year in NCAA Lacrosse.

The modern name arose when French colonists referred to the sticks as "La Crosse" in reference to the staff carried by the Jesuit Bishops back in the 1600's.

The game has always been played for the "Creator" as well as honoring those who had done great things for the tribe, for adding powers to the traditional healing medicines used, for settling disputes, spiritual development and to build stamina in young men. Games would consist of anywhere from 100-1000 men and could last over the course of several days and could cover many miles.

Many of the missionaries had seen these battles and had originally misunderstood what their true meaning was, due to the violence that was sometimes present.

The Commandments of Lacrosse

Over time, the progression of varying stick sizes and shapes has stayed closest to the Iroquois versions, while the shorter or double stick versions of the Great Lakes and Southeastern tribes, respectfully, are not used in the modern game, which started to develop in the early 1800's for men and late 1800's for women.

Today, the women's game is actually closest to the original practices, with little to no equipment, while men's lacrosse players are heavily equipped.

Lacrosse was formerly an Olympic sport in the early 1900's and has continued to grow in regards to the World Games with teams from many countries participating in the sport that developed in North America by the Native American Indian tribes.

You may now watch countries such as Japan, Canada, Wales, Ireland, Germany, Australia, South Korea, Poland, the United States and Bermuda to name a few in addition to the Iroquois National team, who of course represent the Creator and his spirit on and off the field.

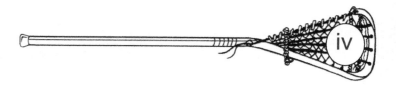

The Commandments of Lacrosse

Lacrosse is considered one of the fastest growing sports in the United States, if not the world, as seen in some of the countries now represented at the world games. Clubs and teams are forming all over the world and if it is not in your town yet, it could be in the very near future.

The Creator's game has been featured in movies like "American Pie" and on TV shows in small bits and clips, though there was never much reference to the creation of the game itself or to it's spiritual nature. This has all changed with the release of "Crooked Arrows" in 2012 which is the first major motion picture featuring and focused around not only the game itself, but the customs and cultures of the Native American people who brought us this game.

As time progresses, rules will continue to be modified to allow Lacrosse to be a sport that is suitable to play at all ages. Many of the rules apply to maintain the safety and health of those participating as it still may be a violent game with physical contact, slashes and foul play when not addressed appropriately as mentioned in the Disclaimer.

The Commandments of Lacrosse

Whether indoor (box) or outdoor (field) lacrosse, there always seems to be a game or tournament happening and thus the game continues to grow. Go grab a stick to participate yourself, or go watch those who are playing and remember, you/they are playing for the Creator.

Enjoy Lacrosse for everything that it was and currently is...And be sure to follow the rules set forth within your league.

Play for the love of the game, then grow the game!

For Boys and Girls Lacrosse

The Commandments of Lacrosse

The Commandments of Lacrosse

Table of Contents

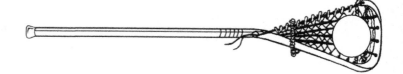

The Commandments of Lacrosse

Commandment #1

"Thou shalt never hit the goalie in the chest when shooting."

Off stick, or weak side, hip is the hardest shot for a goalie to save so you need to learn to pick spots by shooting on the corners and mid-level where the Goalies hips would be.

Practice by hitting the same spot on a wall over and over again, or hang a target in your goal and aim for it with every shot to improve your accuracy.

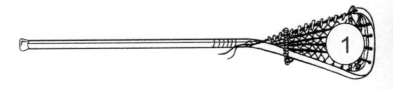

The Commandments of Lacrosse

Commandment #2

"Bounce shots are best."

They are hard to read and rarely bounce true unless on turf and are therefore hard to judge by a goalie. Hit a spot right inside the crease line to make it harder for the goalie to adjust correctly

Combine this with trying to hit the same spot after the bounce. If you bounce too close to the Goalie you risk hitting their legs or being saved with their stick. Bounce outside the crease and you allow them extra time to respond to the shot.

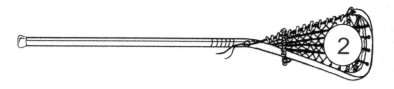

The Commandments of Lacrosse

Commandment #3

"Listen and talk to your stick as you cradle, this will insure good stick protection."

When cradling, you should be bringing your stick back and forth between the area in front of your face and on the side of your helmet or goggles when your stick is in the vertical position.

Do not leave your stick hanging to be checked and become part of a yard sale.

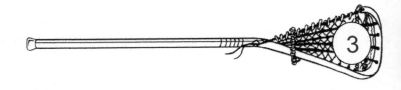

The Commandments of Lacrosse

Commandment #4

"A goal proves that you can beat the goalie; an assist proves that you are smart."

The bigger and faster team does not always win, but the team that plays smarter is often successful.

Understand that Lacrosse is as much a mental game as it is a physical one and make the smart choice when you have the chance to help your team score.

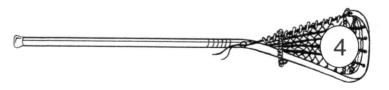

The Commandments of Lacrosse

Commandment #5

"Always look to make the extra pass."

There is always someone else open that might have a better angle or opening on the field.

Do not force the ball, but instead pull it out and settle it down to see where you can make another pass. Be patient!

5

The Commandments of Lacrosse

Commandment #6

"Thou shalt not pass the ball close enough to the goalie or the cage such that the goalie is able to intercept your pass."

This is an unnecessary forcing of the ball. Be patient and work it around until the opening presents itself. Your coach would much rather have you hold onto the ball for a longer possession, than turn it over to the Goalie for a fast break going the opposite direction with players out of position on the attack end.

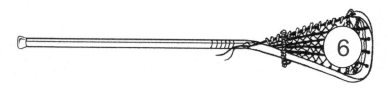

The Commandments of Lacrosse

Commandment #7

"Thou must have the ability to catch <u>and</u> throw with both hands."

You will be a more dynamic player and greater threat if you can go both directions and keep the defensemen on their heels at all times.

If you are a defensemen you will be able to throw checks and clear against the best attack players with ease when you can use both hands.

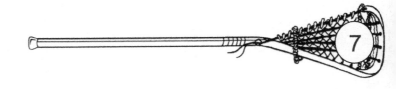

7

The Commandments of Lacrosse

Commandment #8

"Thou must move whenever you do not have the ball; Keep your defenseman confused, thinking and occupied. Remember the words of wisdom from the cavemen: He who stands still, is lunch!"

If you stand still, you also make it easier for your defenseman to slide and double the ball without having to worry about you.

8

The Commandments of Lacrosse

Commandment #9

"Never "telegraph" a pass"

Keep the opponent guessing where you are going with the ball and use your peripheral vision to help you move the ball where you are "not looking".

The Commandments of Lacrosse

Commandment #10

"Thou must practice on the wall in order to be good"

This is a basic skill that you can always improve with, try a new technique or way to play wall ball that you have never done before.

There are many ways you can do this to improve your skill level with both hands...Even the best players spend time "on the wall!"

*See page 59 for related wall ball drills.

The Commandments of Lacrosse

Commandment #11

"Thou shalt always move to a passed ball; never stand still to wait for a pass to come to you."

Don't wait for the ball to come to you, instead be aggressive and attack the ball so that no one else takes it from you.

Often you are able to catch it instead of letting it become a wild bounce pass that goes out of bounds and become an unnecessary turnover.

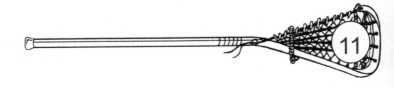

The Commandments of Lacrosse

Commandment #12

"The best players pick up the ground balls"

Get both hands low and parallel to the ground, NO ONE HANDED GB's.

Run through the ball like a bull charging a red flag.

Aim to be the ball hawk of your team everyday.

*See Page 53 on Winning the GB WAR

The Commandments of Lacrosse

Commandment #13

"Vee in and Vee out in order to get open for a pass."

Create a disturbance and commotion in the group so your defender does not know whether you are going towards the cage or away from it to create open space between you and them.

Those on offense who keep moving will get open with a little patience. If it does not work the first time, try it again until it does.

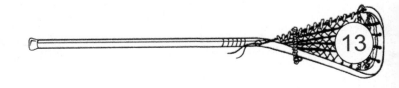

The Commandments of Lacrosse

Commandment #14

"Never get caught off-sides."

This is playing smart and prevents turnovers. The opposite midfielder on the far side is often responsible for this, especially when a defender is bringing the ball up field.

"Middie Back, Middie Back" should be called when the defender is going over the midfield line into the attack end. The same holds true to the restraining line in the women's game.

On a ground ball situation, do not cross the line to grab the ball should it come towards you there, though reach with your stick as long as you do not step on the line!

The Commandments of Lacrosse

Commandment #15

"Check on the head of your opponents stick."

Poke and slap checks work the best here, while you should stay away from the body as much as possible.

Patience and timing in your checks can work much better than being a hack and prevents injuries and unnecessary penalties which also harm your team.

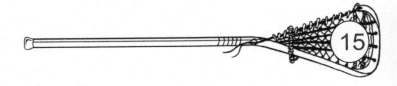

The Commandments of Lacrosse

Commandment #16

"Thou shalt always congratulate your teammates; You are, and can do nothing without them."

This is a TEAM sport and they may create opportunities that allow you to score later in the game or in future games.

Teamwork makes the dream work!

The Commandments of Lacrosse

Commandment #17

"Thou shalt always keep your head up; don't look at the ball inside your stick."

If you are looking at the ball, you do not know what is going on around you or where the opponent is. Become comfortable and get use to the feeling of the ball in your stick.

Carry your stick around the house and cradle with both hands to become familiar with the weight of the stick and ball together.

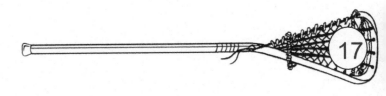

The Commandments of Lacrosse

Commandment #18

"Always stay in front of your fellow midfielders on a fast break. They will not be able to pass to you if you are behind them."

Hustle up field on offense as well as hustle back to get in the hole on defense if your opponent is staying ahead of the ball as well.

The Commandments of Lacrosse

Commandment #19

"If the goalie comes out of the cage, turn him/her to their weak hand by shutting off his/her strong hand side."

Often goalies do not get as much practice using both hands because of reaction time limitations in the cage, so they favor one direction more than other.

If you are a goalie, make sure you improve your weak hand to be able to clear the ball better.

The Commandments of Lacrosse

Commandment #20

"Never, never, never hang your stick."

It is not a piece of luggage you are carrying around waiting to be checked away, unless you want a yard sale to take place and the ball to go in the opposite direction.

A defensemen with patience and timing will strip the ball from this player with ease.

The Commandments of Lacrosse

Commandment #21

"Always be alert of your mark and the ball's position when you are on defense."

Do not get caught ball watching, but you must know where the ball is at all times so you can maintain proper positioning on the field.

Your coach may say "keep your head on a swivel" which means to be moving your head around in all directions to know what is happening all over the field.

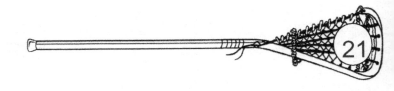

The Commandments of Lacrosse

Commandment #22

"Thou shalt play the 'Ball-You-Man' triangle."

Just like in other sports, you want to create the better angles to be able to cut off the ball and defend the person at the same time.

Lining up wrong can result in getting beat, so be sure to always find a good position to help out.

The Commandments of Lacrosse

Commandment #23

"Thou shalt always be ready to slide to a teammate to help him/her on defense."

Make sure you are calling out that you have their back and are "hot" or "I'm 1" so they know where their weak side help is coming from.

A good defense will rotate when you slide so all players get picked up again and prevent the team from attacking the goal further.

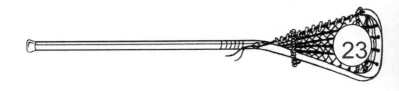

The Commandments of Lacrosse

Commandment #24

"You have a stick, use it: check."

If the ball is flying through the air, or you are up at the midfield waiting for a ground ball to come, you need to check their stick to prevent your opponent from getting the ball.

In girls lacrosse you must be careful here as you can get called with an "empty" if you hit their stick without the ball present. Boxing out your mark will allow you to grab the front spot closer to the ball in this scenario.

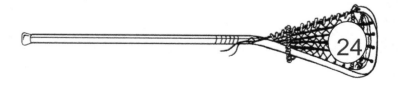

The Commandments of Lacrosse

Commandment #25

"Use your stick not as a caveman's club or ax, but as a surgeon's scalpel."

Basic Checks work many times more than the fancy checks which instead usually end up drawing a flag with penalty time. You want to make it as simple as possible so the ball comes out and you can pick it up.

Do not get caught up in the idea that you landed a home run check only to stare at the ball being picked up again by the person you stripped originally.

The Commandments of Lacrosse

Commandment #26

"Don't lunge at the offensive player, be balanced, wait for his move."

Have an open stance with legs about shoulder width apart, knees bent slightly, hips facing the opponent and stick pointing towards them as well or angled slightly upwards to block a pass or feeding attempt.

Your feet should be moving so you can adjust and go either way with the player. Be sure to focus on their hips and numbers. If you follow their arms or stick, you will be swinging and running all over the place getting beat.

The Commandments of Lacrosse

Commandment #27

"Thou shalt not allow the offensive player to crowd or push you. If they are too close, push them out"

You have a right to the space as well, so keep them moving out of the way of your "House". They are an unwelcomed guest that you want to keep from getting any further.

The Commandments of Lacrosse

Commandment #28

"Thou shall be intimidating on defense"

Bark, talk loudly and talk often to show the offense you mean business.

Come out when they catch the ball, break down and say "me, me, me" or Ball, I got Ball etc. with a nice poke check to show them you are going to battle them until you get the ball back and head the other way.

In the girls game, time your slap check on the head of your opponents stick if they are hanging it for you to check it. Be controlled though with a quick down and up checking motion.

The Commandments of Lacrosse

Commandment #29

"If your mark beats you and there has been a slide, go to the hole and pick up a player"

Never stand still and always try to find the open player.

Your teammates picked up where you got beat, now back them up as well. You will pay them back later by backing them up when the ball comes from the other side.

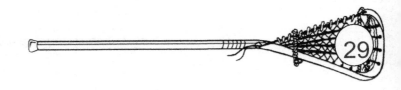

The Commandments of Lacrosse

Commandment #30

"Always talk and communicate. The best players are talkers"

Those who are vocal often control the game and can be intimidating to those who are quiet and do not talk as much.

Your talking on defense can also throw off the concentration of those on offense who are trying to run a play.

On offense be vocal so you know who is going where, when you are setting up a play.

The Commandments of Lacrosse

Commandment #31

"Choke up on your stick if you have difficulty handling it"

Find a position that is comfortable for catching and one for throwing (they should not necessarily be the same), but be sure to protect your "butt end" so as to not be hanging your stick, especially for long sticks running down the field clearing the ball in the men's game.

Wrapping a narrow piece of athletic tape around these spots where your bottom hand should stop or rest, will help you easily find your balance spots when you are on the run and can not look to see where your hands are.

The Commandments of Lacrosse

Commandment #32

"After picking up a ground ball, put it to your face, and run to an open area"

Protection is a key factor in maintaining control of the ball. You must value it and not hang your stick afterwards to let it get stripped away, then start talking and listening to your stick until you are out of traffic and have found someone to move the ball to.

You should be looking for an open person as soon as you pick the ball up to move it away from you and the congested area.

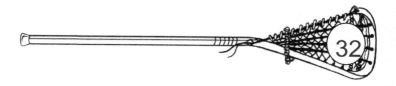

The Commandments of Lacrosse

Commandment #33

"Defensemen, stay tight on the fast break"

If you spread out, this makes the rotations harder and the scoring opportunities easier as there is more space between defensemen, goalie and the goal.

Talk is a must here and you must always get back in the hole and continue until the midfielders come and you are all even.

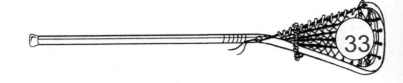

The Commandments of Lacrosse

Commandment #34

"Every time the ball moves, you must move"

Do not stand still or you will get beat on defense, or you will never get the ball on offense.

You should always be re-positioning yourself to accept a pass or to make a pick for someone else to accept a pass. If you are on offense, it will keep you ready and knowing what is happening.

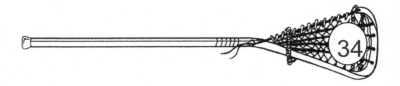

The Commandments of Lacrosse

Commandment #35

"Stay intense by anticipating what the team will do next"

Always be ready for their next move...Feel a defender who may be sliding early, so that you may pop open on the defensive end, or put more pressure on someone cutting to minimize their chance of receiving the ball.

The Commandments of Lacrosse

Commandment #36

"If you double team, do so with authority; ask yourself, do I want to be a hammer or a nail?"

When you double, you leave your man open behind you in a likely position that they may get the ball and get a shot off.

Make sure you are talking through this so someone knows they must back you up and others know you are coming to double the ball and can figure out which way to force the opponent so they will "turn into" the double team.

The Commandments of Lacrosse

Commandment #37

"Great defensemen, like great offensive players, see the entire field: keep your head up when you're clearing the ball. Impress fans with your smarts"

There is nothing more exciting than seeing a defensemen bringing the ball up field and putting a shot in the net. They must be aware of where everyone is so that can make the split second decision to pass the ball off and get back over the line, or if they should continue towards the goal and take a shot. A nice long pass from the end line often starts off a fast break that leads to a crowd raising goal.

The Commandments of Lacrosse

Commandment #38

"Keep players out of the funnel"

This is the area in front of the cage! You want them to run around as much as possible, but not coming closer into your zone. Force them out and around and be sure to stick close to cutters so that you may prevent them from receiving a feed from behind.

The "Check" call is crucial from goalies/teammates here as the defender may not always see where the ball is if he is following the cutter.

The Commandments of Lacrosse

Commandment #39

"Thou shalt be economic with your checks"

Don't waste a lot of time and energy on fancy checks. Throw them when you know you have a high percentage chance of landing them and causing a turnover.

The poke check is the most important to use and requires little energy. You can be a jack hammer with this and still not put yourself out of balance or give up position.

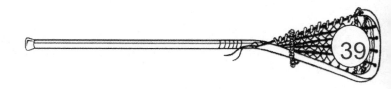

Commandment #40

"Great defensemen do not take the ball away, they prevent their opponent from scoring."

Being in the correct position often causes an attack player to move the ball along and not force the issue of trying to score. Nothing fancy is needed, just be in the right space at the right time and if presented with an opportunity to check, then be sure to take it.

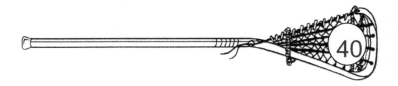

The Commandments of Lacrosse

Commandment #41

"Love the game and play and practice with passion. Ask your coach for magazines, books, and tips. Be a student of the game"

The more you learn, the better you will become.

Watch games on TV or of a higher level and focus on your position to see what the best person at that level does. Get ideas from other positions as well and become an all around player who "Respects the Game"

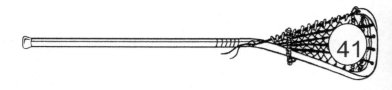

The Commandments of Lacrosse

Commandment #42

"A great man once said, "Nothing great was ever achieved without enthusiasm." In other words, give everything your all."

Leave it all on the field.

Do not come back later wishing you did something different...'no regrets' should be all that is on your mind as you did everything you could each day out and have the attitude of "being all in" with the team and your progress.

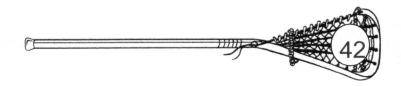

The Commandments of Lacrosse

Commandment #43

"The saying "Practice makes perfect" is incorrect. "Perfect practice makes perfect!"

Repetition is key in any facet of life to make something easier or happen with relative ease. The pros make it looks so easy, because they have become experts at failure and know how to do it the right way.

Learn from your mistakes until it becomes normal. Training your muscles to do certain movements in practice carries over into the games to look fluid as though you were a natural.

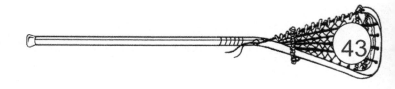

The Commandments of Lacrosse

Commandment #44

"When in a game, thou shalt never dispute a call or argue with an official for any reason!"

The only person to talk to an official is the coach, or captain. The officials are human and can not see everything that occurs on the field. Many times it is a judgment call on their part (whether correct or not) and they should not be ridiculed by a player ever.

Lacrosse is played as a game in current times and should not have life bearing consequences where a ref's call will determine your fate forever. Get over it and accept it for what it was, learn from it and move on to make a better play later.

44

The Commandments of Lacrosse

Commandment #45

"Thou shalt always know the score of the game"

"You got to be in it to win it" and should always know what is going on. It is only a few hours of your life, so pay close attention to what is happening in the game...Have FOCUS!

Regardless of score, you should always give it your all throughout the game. No letdowns. A complete game is needed for success. A short letdown can be costly.

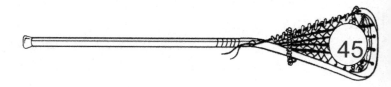

The Commandments of Lacrosse

Commandment #46

"Thou shalt encourage and uplift your teammates who are not playing well"

Everyone has an off day, or someone might be at a level below your skill level.

If you want them to be successful in helping your team achieve the goals set forth in the beginning of the season, you need to help them out when they may be making a mistake or playing below the expectations of the program.

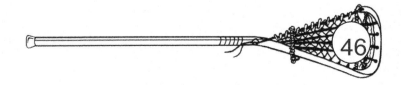

The Commandments of Lacrosse

Commandment #47

"When coached or told to do something in a practice, ask <u>yourself</u> why? You may then come to a better understanding of the game"

Not the "palms up" sort of why, but the serious kind where you think about what the coach is telling you.

In most cases your coach has played at many levels and had great coaches himself and might actually know a thing or two about the game that can help you improve yours.

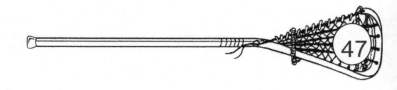

The Commandments of Lacrosse

Commandment #48

"Always have your equipment ready prior to a game"

Don't be the person who shows up without a major piece of equipment like a helmet or glove. A simple rule of thumb for the school team is that you do not leave the locker room without all your equipment on and you get on the bus this way if necessary for a game. The same for the ride home and entering the locker...make sure it is all on.

For those on summer and club teams with no locker room, make sure you have some method or type of gear that will help you in bringing all your equipment to the next practice or game.

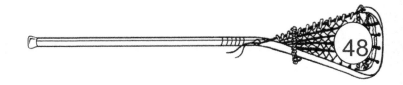

The Commandments of Lacrosse

Commandment #49

"Accept the responsibilities of being an athlete: work hard in school, represent your family, community, and team with pride and honor"

Remember, you are a student first and an athlete last. Playing sports is a privilege which can be taken away easily when the school, family and community commitments are not met. Be a person of good character and make wise decisions. Think first and act second in regards to how your response to a situation will affect your teammates and family.

The Commandments of Lacrosse

Commandment #50

"Practice, practice, practice, then practice some more"

You will never be perfect, but you can aim to achieve perfection by putting the time in at practice and after practice as well with wall ball, ground ball drills, shooting on a goal, playing catch, performing stick tricks and much more!

As stated earlier, "Perfect Practice makes Perfect!" and should be followed with all safety guidelines in place so that no one gets hurt. You might master a great check, but it should not be at the expense of an opponent, who could be injured in the process.

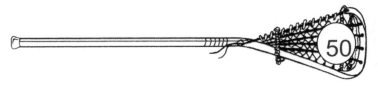

The Commandments of Lacrosse

Bonus Commandment #51

"Thou shalt refer back to this book over and over again until these commandments become instilled in your game and way of life"

Just like practice, you never learn something outright the first time. Repetition is needed. The second time you read these, you will pick up something new, or one of the commandments will have a new meaning for you.

Your interpretations at the beginning of the season will be different from the end as well.

The Commandments of Lacrosse Survey and Staying in Touch

Please take a moment to complete our online survey to help develop future editions of the book and other products to help your Lacrosse game:

TAKE THIS LACROSSE SURVEY→ tinyurl.com/lacrossesurvey

You can also stay in touch with Basic Lacrosse at the following places:

Facebook→ Facebook.com/BasicLacrosse
Twitter→   Twitter.com/BasicLacrosse
Blog→   BasicLacrosse.com/blog
Email→   DaveGardner@BasicLacrosse.com
Instagram→Instagram.com/SuperDaveGardner
Store→   BasicLacrosse.com

Email or send us your lacrosse stories and you might find it in the next edition of our book.

Basic Lacrosse: Attn Dave Gardner
110 Gulino Ave
Camillus, NY 13031

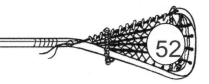

52

The Commandments of Lacrosse

FREE Bonus Ground Ball Report

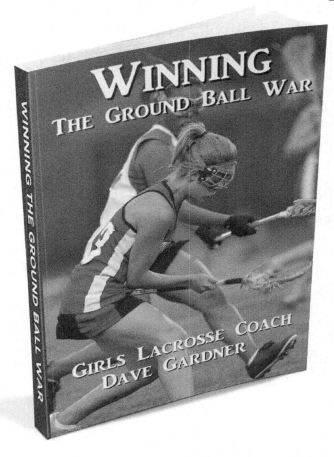

Grab Your Free Report HERE:

"GroundBallWar.com"

The Commandments of Lacrosse

The Lacrosse Powershaft

Basic Lacrosse is an official Lacrosse distributor for the Lacrosse Powershaft. If you want to shoot faster, throw farther, check harder or have better speed with face-offs, draw or goalie saves, the Powershaft is for you and comes in many lengths and weights.

Grab your Lacrosse Powershaft and see training videos as well as player testimonials at:

"LacrossePowershaft.com"

or contact DaveGardner@BasicLacrosse.com for larger team orders

54

*The Powershaft is to be used for Training purposes only.

Other Suggested Lacrosse Reading

The Spirit in the Stick is a novels that follows a 200 year history of a hand crafted Native American lacrosse stick that is handed down generation after generation. Within each passing of the stick to the succeeding guarding, each person gains the "Spirit" from the previous guardian. This easy to read piece of fiction brings you from the battle field to the lacrosse field and will be enjoyed by all those who have played or just love the game of lacrosse.

Grab *The Spirit in the Stick* novel today at:
"LacrosseBooks.com"

or contact DaveGardner@BasicLacrosse.com for larger team orders

55

The Commandments of Lacrosse
About the Author

Dave Gardner currently teaches Chemistry in Central New York at the Solvay School District, which currently does not have a lacrosse program He has therefore been coaching at surrounding schools and has spent time coaching both boys and girls lacrosse over the years.

Dave is a Returned Peace Corps Volunteer, having served in the Solomon Islands from 1998-2000. He holds his Masters of Arts in Teaching from SUNY Cortland and also has a developing online and local marketing business.

Dave lives in Camillus, NY with has three daughters who keep him busy when he is not teaching and coaching.

You can let Dave know what you think about the 50 Commandments of Lacrosse by sending him an email at DaveGardner@BasicLacrosse.com

Better yet, leave him an easy video testimonial here: LacrosseCommandments.com/Blog/bookreview

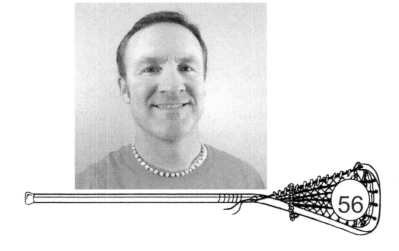

56

The Commandments of Lacrosse

One of the best things that ever happened to me was being cut from the Varsity lacrosse team during my Junior year at West Genesee High School in the Spring of 1992. I had played baseball and lacrosse growing up and settled on lacrosse during my sophomore year. You can see more of the story how I got here at LacrosseCommandments.com.

Not putting the correct time in, I was not up to par my Junior year and did not make the team. Coaches Messere and Deegan instead presented me with the opportunity to coach and that year I spent the season as the modified assistant lacrosse coach, which turned me onto coaching forever.

I practiced every day from that point on and as a Senior, made the varsity team, when they could have picked a younger player over me. I later continued my love for the sport at Cortland State University where I was a member of the Red Dragons lacrosse team all four years I was there.

Since graduating college and bringing lacrosse sticks with me in travels to Belize, The Solomon Islands and Kenya to continue spreading my love for the game that has provided me with many opportunities, I have also continued to coach the game.

The Commandments of Lacrosse

I have coached both boys modified (7th-9thgrade) and girls JV and Varsity lacrosse for over 15 years in addition to coaching the first of my three daughters in the 3rd/4th and 5th/6th grade levels before she started modified lax.

I will always strive to present the basics of lacrosse, which is why I originally decided to call my website "BasicLacrosse.com" and why I will run a drill sometimes longer than a player may be "use to" until I see it working right. Perfect Practice Makes Perfect, right!

My coaching philosophy will continue in this manner as I will teach the basics of lacrosse, just like those taught to me back in the 1980's when I first started playing in the summer developmental leagues at Shove Park in Camillus, NY.

Finally, I would like to thank Coach Chris Kenneally, who was like a second father growing up and who gave me my first stick and introduced me to the game of lacrosse when I was 6. He was also very understanding over the years as I broke parts of his fence shooting on the goal!

"You get out of it what you put into it!"

-Dave Gardner-

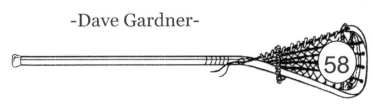

The Commandments of Lacrosse

Did you play wall ball today?

Set a specified amount of time each day to play wall ball and keep track of how many times you hit the wall each day and as you improve you will find that you are increasing your repetitions in the same amount of time.

Another way could be to do a set number of tosses and as you improve you will have to spend less time completing the task. Then you can spend the extra time doing more complex tosses or variations of tosses.

When you get comfortable, add sand or filler to your shaft to add resistance to your passes and when you use a regular stick you will be amazed at how well you can throw the ball (See the Powershaft pg 54)

The Commandments of Lacrosse
Basic Wall Ball Drills

Throw Right	→	Catch Right
Throw Left	→	Catch Left
Throw Right	→	Catch Left
Throw Left	→	Catch Right
Throw Right	→	Catch Cross Handed on left side
Throw Left	→	Catch Cross Handed on right side
Throw Cross Handed L	→	Catch Right
Throw Cross Handed R	→	Catch Left
Behind the back Right	→	Catch Right
Behind the back Left	→	Catch Left

Do these drills at various distances from a wall or partner. Starting out at shorter distances and then creating more space between you and the wall and/or partner.

You can also do these same drills with bouncing between you and the wall to create a larger variety, where you can either bounce on the ground first, then hit the wall, or hit the wall first and then allow to hit the ground.

Remember, you get out of it what you put into it!

See My sample series of 18 Wall Ball drills on Youtube! Just search for "Lacrosse Commandments Wall Ball Video" and you should see a series of videos to learn from! Be sure to leave a comment if you watch a video! Or go to "LacrosseCommandments.com/WallBall"

The Commandments of Lacrosse

The "One Player One Book" Movement

Doing a fundraiser? Providing Senior night gifts? Perhaps you have a Lax Store yourself...or want to help share the game around the world, well here is your chance!

Head on over to the website and be able to help out players from all over! Go to "OnePlayerOneBook.com" to order a set for your teammates, your own players and parents or even to donate in another country.

Our goal is to have every lacrosse player get a copy of this book to have for themselves.

Feel free to share the spreading of the book as well with other lax fans who may be interested.

OnePlayerOneBook.com
Or
1Player1Book.com

The Commandments of Lacrosse

Want a Free Digital Copy of the Book for Purchasing this Physical Copy?

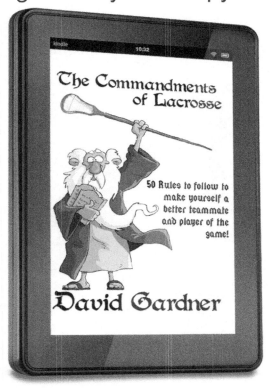

Just register your account FREE at
Lacrossecommandments.com/Blog/free-copy/

Note: Case Sensitive

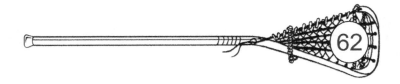

62

The Commandments of Lacrosse

Now available in Audio! Grab it at
"LacrosseCommandments.com/Audio"

Note: Case sensitive

Listen on your Smartphone on the way to the game, from home on your computer or anywhere you can access the internet and learn!

63

The Commandments of Lacrosse

Strength Training For Lacrosse

As I went though high school, college and even as a coach, I realized I hated working out for long periods of time…Heck I would rather be on the wall or on the field playing and I am sure you do as well, though there is something to be said about improvements in strength for your overall game growth.

I started focusing on just one major muscle group every other day and gave lots of rest between sessions which allowed for ample muscle recovery, repair and growth and saw great gains in my strength when I pushed myself to failure in these workouts. Less is more when it came to building my muscles!

This recommendation does not come as a lacrosse skill improvement right away, though these workouts can do wonders for your overall health and presence in the game. It is even family friendly to do workouts together and have a spotter with you to push you harder and reach true muscle failure. You can find out more about this great program that I work with at

"7MinuteMuscles.com"

Workouts/Protein Supplements and more!

64

The Commandments of Lacrosse

Thank you for taking the time to read the *Commandments of Lacrosse*. Be sure to read them a couple times and tell others about it so they can also benefit from these strategies and grab a copy as well.

Remember, you get out of it what you put into it!

On the next pages of this book edition you will find a Journal to keep track of your skill improvement and growth in lacrosse. (If you are reading the digital version, feel free to print these pages out for your personal reference and success.)

Record a summary each day of the types of drills or workout you completed and how long it took to complete it. You should start to see your repetitions go up while the time it takes to do this should go down, especially with wall-ball drills.

It is not always what you do, as much as what you do daily that makes the difference in your growth!

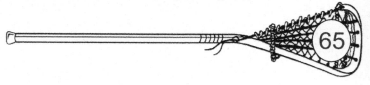

65

The Commandments of Lacrosse
Your Daily Lax Journal

Wall Ball I Running I Arms I Legs I Mental I Play I Watch I Read

Monday

Tuesday

Wednesday

Thursday

Friday

Saturday

Sunday

66

The Commandments of Lacrosse
Your Daily Lax Journal

Wall Ball **I** Running **I** Arms **I** Legs **I** Mental **I** Play **I** Watch **I** Read

Monday

Tuesday

Wednesday

Thursday

Friday

Saturday

Sunday

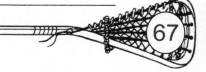

The Commandments of Lacrosse
Your Daily Lax Journal

Wall Ball I Running I Arms I Legs I Mental I Play I Watch I Read

Monday

Tuesday

Wednesday

Thursday

Friday

Saturday

Sunday

The Commandments of Lacrosse
Your Daily Lax Journal

Wall Ball **I** Running **I** Arms **I** Legs **I** Mental **I** Play **I** Watch **I** Read

Monday

Tuesday

Wednesday

Thursday

Friday

Saturday

Sunday

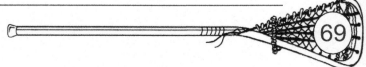

69

The Commandments of Lacrosse
Your Daily Lax Journal

Wall Ball **I** Running **I** Arms **I** Legs **I** Mental **I** Play **I** Watch **I** Read

Monday

Tuesday

Wednesday

Thursday

Friday

Saturday

Sunday

70

The Commandments of Lacrosse
Your Daily Lax Journal

Wall Ball **I** Running **I** Arms **I** Legs **I** Mental **I** Play **I** Watch **I** Read

Monday

Tuesday

Wednesday

Thursday

Friday

Saturday

Sunday

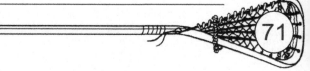

The Commandments of Lacrosse
Your Daily Lax Journal

Wall Ball I Running I Arms I Legs I Mental I Play I Watch I Read

Monday

_____

Tuesday

_____

Wednesday

_____

Thursday

_____

Friday

_____

Saturday

_____

Sunday

_____

72

The Commandments of Lacrosse
Your Daily Lax Journal

Wall Ball **I** Running **I** Arms **I** Legs **I** Mental **I** Play **I** Watch **I** Read

Monday

Tuesday

Wednesday

Thursday

Friday

Saturday

Sunday

The Commandments of Lacrosse
Your Daily Lax Journal

Wall Ball I Running I Arms I Legs I Mental I Play I Watch I Read

Monday

Tuesday

Wednesday

Thursday

Friday

Saturday

Sunday

74

The Commandments of Lacrosse
Your Daily Lax Journal

Wall Ball **I** Running **I** Arms **I** Legs **I** Mental **I** Play **I** Watch **I** Read

Monday

Tuesday

Wednesday

Thursday

Friday

Saturday

Sunday

75

The Commandments of Lacrosse
Your Daily Lax Journal

Wall Ball I Running I Arms I Legs I Mental I Play I Watch I Read

Monday

Tuesday

Wednesday

Thursday

Friday

Saturday

Sunday

The Commandments of Lacrosse
Your Daily Lax Journal

Wall Ball | Running | Arms | Legs | Mental | Play | Watch | Read

Monday

Tuesday

Wednesday

Thursday

Friday

Saturday

Sunday

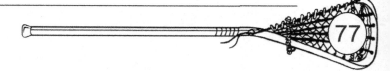

The Commandments of Lacrosse
Your Daily Lax Journal

Wall Ball I Running I Arms I Legs I Mental I Play I Watch I Read

Monday

Tuesday

Wednesday

Thursday

Friday

Saturday

Sunday

78

The Commandments of Lacrosse
Your Daily Lax Journal

Wall Ball I Running I Arms I Legs I Mental I Play I Watch I Read

Monday

Tuesday

Wednesday

Thursday

Friday

Saturday

Sunday

The Commandments of Lacrosse
Your Daily Lax Journal

Wall Ball **I** Running **I** Arms **I** Legs **I** Mental **I** Play **I** Watch **I** Read

Monday

Tuesday

Wednesday

Thursday

Friday

Saturday

Sunday

80

The Commandments of Lacrosse
Your Daily Lax Journal

Wall Ball I Running I Arms I Legs I Mental I Play I Watch I Read

Monday

Tuesday

Wednesday

Thursday

Friday

Saturday

Sunday

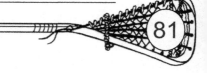

81

The Commandments of Lacrosse
Your Daily Lax Journal

Wall Ball I Running I Arms I Legs I Mental I Play I Watch I Read

Monday

Tuesday

Wednesday

Thursday

Friday

Saturday

Sunday

82

The Commandments of Lacrosse
Your Daily Lax Journal

Wall Ball I Running I Arms I Legs I Mental I Play I Watch I Read

Monday

Tuesday

Wednesday

Thursday

Friday

Saturday

Sunday

The Commandments of Lacrosse
Your Daily Lax Journal

Wall Ball I Running I Arms I Legs I Mental I Play I Watch I Read

Monday

Tuesday

Wednesday

Thursday

Friday

Saturday

Sunday

84

The Commandments of Lacrosse
Your Daily Lax Journal

Wall Ball I Running I Arms I Legs I Mental I Play I Watch I Read

Monday

Tuesday

Wednesday

Thursday

Friday

Saturday

Sunday

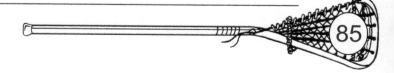
85

The Commandments of Lacrosse
Your Daily Lax Journal

Wall Ball **I** Running **I** Arms **I** Legs **I** Mental **I** Play **I** Watch **I** Read

Monday

Tuesday

Wednesday

Thursday

Friday

Saturday

Sunday

86

The Commandments of Lacrosse
Your Daily Lax Journal

Wall Ball **I** Running **I** Arms **I** Legs **I** Mental **I** Play **I** Watch **I** Read

Monday

Tuesday

Wednesday

Thursday

Friday

Saturday

Sunday

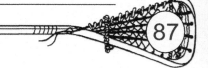

87

The Commandments of Lacrosse
Your Daily Lax Journal

Wall Ball I Running I Arms I Legs I Mental I Play I Watch I Read

Monday

Tuesday

Wednesday

Thursday

Friday

Saturday

Sunday

88

The Commandments of Lacrosse
Your Daily Lax Journal

Wall Ball **I** Running **I** Arms **I** Legs **I** Mental **I** Play **I** Watch **I** Read

Monday

Tuesday

Wednesday

Thursday

Friday

Saturday

Sunday

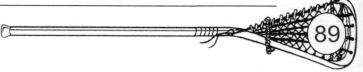

The Commandments of Lacrosse
Your Daily Lax Journal

Wall Ball I Running I Arms I Legs I Mental I Play I Watch I Read

Monday

Tuesday

Wednesday

Thursday

Friday

Saturday

Sunday

90

The Commandments of Lacrosse
Your Daily Lax Journal

Wall Ball **I** Running **I** Arms **I** Legs **I** Mental **I** Play **I** Watch **I** Read

Monday

Tuesday

Wednesday

Thursday

Friday

Saturday

Sunday

The Commandments of Lacrosse
Your Daily Lax Journal

Wall Ball **I** Running I Arms I Legs I Mental I Play I Watch I Read

Monday

_____

Tuesday

_____

Wednesday

_____

Thursday

_____

Friday

_____

Saturday

_____

Sunday

_____

92

The Commandments of Lacrosse
Your Daily Lax Journal

Wall Ball I Running I Arms I Legs I Mental I Play I Watch I Read

Monday

Tuesday

Wednesday

Thursday

Friday

Saturday

Sunday

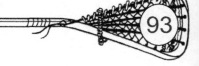

93

The Commandments of Lacrosse

Your Daily Lax Journal

Wall Ball **I** Running **I** Arms **I** Legs **I** Mental **I** Play **I** Watch **I** Read

Monday

Tuesday

Wednesday

Thursday

Friday

Saturday

Sunday

94

The Commandments of Lacrosse
Your Daily Lax Journal

Wall Ball **I** Running **I** Arms **I** Legs **I** Mental **I** Play **I** Watch **I** Read

Monday

Tuesday

Wednesday

Thursday

Friday

Saturday

Sunday

The Commandments of Lacrosse
Your Daily Lax Journal

Wall Ball I Running I Arms I Legs I Mental I Play I Watch I Read

Monday

Tuesday

Wednesday

Thursday

Friday

Saturday

Sunday

96

The Commandments of Lacrosse
Your Daily Lax Journal

Wall Ball **I** Running **I** Arms **I** Legs **I** Mental **I** Play **I** Watch **I** Read

Monday

Tuesday

Wednesday

Thursday

Friday

Saturday

Sunday

The Commandments of Lacrosse
Your Daily Lax Journal

Wall Ball **I** Running **I** Arms **I** Legs **I** Mental **I** Play **I** Watch **I** Read

Monday

_____

Tuesday

_____

Wednesday

_____

Thursday

_____

Friday

_____

Saturday

_____

Sunday

_____

The Commandments of Lacrosse

Last Word

The only way to keep growing your skills and the game of lacrosse is to take action!

Get out there and play.

Share the game with others.

Be passionate about the sport, though be sure to enjoy other sports as well, to become a well rounded athlete. There are many sports which will help you to become a better player, harder hitter, faster cutter and team player, so always think how you can incorporate what you learn in one sport into the sport of lacrosse.

-Dave Gardner-

Leave us a review here:
LacrosseCommandments.com/Blog/bookreview

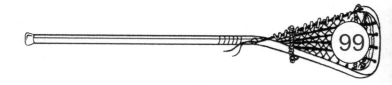

99